BENJAMIN WHITE

READING SKILLS HANDBOOK

Unlocking Successful Reading Strategies

Published in 2023 by Amba Press, Melbourne, Australia
www.ambapress.com.au

© Benjamin White 2023

All rights reserved. No part of this book may be reproduced or transmitted in any form or by any means, electronic or mechanical, including photocopying, recording or by any information storage and retrieval system, without prior permission in writing from the publisher.

Cover design: Tess McCabe
Editor: Rica Dearman

ISBN: 9781922607027 (pbk)
ISBN: 9781922607034 (ebk)

A catalogue record for this book is available from the National Library of Australia.

Contents

Introduction   1

Reading is fundamental   3

Chapter 1	Understanding reading	4
Chapter 2	The basics of reading comprehension	9
Chapter 3	Developing your vocabulary	14

Reading at school   19

Chapter 4	Reading strategies for textbooks	20
Chapter 5	Reading strategies for literature	25
Chapter 6	Reading strategies for Maths	31
Chapter 7	Reading strategies for Science	35

Reading in the real world   42

Chapter 8	Critical reading skills	43
Chapter 9	Reading in the digital age	49
Chapter 10	Improving reading speed and efficiency	57
Chapter 11	Developing a reading habit	62

Conclusion   66

Introduction

Reading is one of the most important skills. It is essential for success in not only high school, but life. This book, *Reading Skills Handbook*, is written with you, a teenager going through high school, in mind. I've written this based on my years of teaching in the classroom and have included activities that I have used time and time again to help people exactly like you get to grips with reading.

The aim of this book is to help you improve your reading skills in a variety of areas, including:

- Understanding the basics of reading comprehension.
- Developing your vocabulary.
- Learning effective reading strategies for different types of texts.
- Improving your reading speed and efficiency.
- Developing a lifelong reading habit.

I've divided this book into three parts:

1. **Reading is fundamental** covers the basics of reading, including what it means to read effectively.

2. **Reading at school** focuses on specific reading strategies for different types of school texts, such as textbooks, literature, math problems and science articles.

3. **Reading in the real world** explores the importance of critical reading skills, reading in the digital age and developing a lifelong reading habit.

Like I said, each chapter includes an activity to help you practise and apply the skills you learn. So, whether you're a struggling reader, want to improve your reading skills or your parents have bought this book and are forcing you to use it, *Reading Skills Handbook* will help you to reach your full potential. Or, at the very least, help you pass your next assessment.

Reading is fundamental

CHAPTER 1

Understanding reading

IN THIS CHAPTER

The science behind reading
Different types of reading

We all know that reading is a complex skill, but it is essential for academic success and for participating in society. In this chapter, we will explore the science behind reading, debunk some common myths about reading and discuss different types of reading.

The science behind reading

Reading is a cognitive process that involves the brain's visual and linguistic systems working together. When we read, our eyes take in the text and send signals to the brain. The brain then decodes the text into words, which are then linked with their corresponding meanings. This process is incredibly fast and efficient, and it happens without us even thinking about it.

Scientists have learned a lot about the science of reading in recent years. We now know that there are specific areas of the brain that are involved in reading, and that these areas become more active when we read difficult text. We also know that reading skills can be improved through practice and instruction.

Different types of reading

There are different types of reading strategies that can be used for different purposes. These strategies include:

- **Silent reading:** This is the most common type of reading, where we read quietly to ourselves. It is often used for learning, absorbing information and reading for pleasure.

- **Reading aloud:** This involves pronouncing the words out loud, either individually or in a group. It is beneficial for improving pronunciation, fluency and auditory comprehension.

- **Skimming:** This is a method of rapidly looking over a text to get a general sense of its content. We often use skimming to quickly decide if a text is worth reading in detail.

- **Scanning:** This is a reading strategy used to find specific information in a text. Unlike skimming, which provides a broader overview, scanning involves looking for keywords, dates, names or other particular details.

- **Deep reading:** This is an intensive reading strategy that involves close attention to the text, often accompanied by critical thinking and analysis. Deep reading is used when you need to thoroughly understand a text, such as when studying for an exam or reading a complex novel or scientific article.

As mentioned, reading is a complex skill that can be improved through practice and instruction. By understanding the science of reading, debunking common misconceptions and becoming familiar with different reading strategies, you can become a more effective reader.

Activity: Reading styles scavenger hunt

Learning intention: To practise and understand the different types of reading strategies: silent reading, reading aloud, skimming scanning and deep reading.

Instructions:

1. **Materials required:** Gather a variety of texts (textbooks, newspapers, novels, magazines, etc.), a highlighter, a stopwatch or timer.

2. **Step one – Silent reading and reading aloud:** Choose a short piece of text. Spend five minutes reading it silently. Write down the main points you gather during your silent reading. Now read the same piece out loud. Note any information or insights you gain for reading aloud.

3. **Step two – Skimming and scanning:** Pick a newspaper article or a textbook chapter. Spend two minutes skimming the text and write down the main ideas or topics covered. Then, make a list of specific keywords or phrases (such as names, dates or technical terms). Spend another two minutes scanning the text for these keywords. Highlight them as you find them.

4. **Step three – Deep reading:** Choose a short but complex text, such as a scientific article or literary poem. Spend 10–15 minutes deeply reading the text. Write down the main ideas, any questions you have, interesting quotes or unfamiliar words. Try to analyse the text: What is the author's purpose? What strategies do they use to convey their ideas?

5. **Reflection:** Reflect on the process. Which strategy was the easiest for you? Which was the hardest? When might you use each of these strategies in real-life situations?

Extension: Presentation

Knowledge is power. So share that power with your friends by preparing a brief presentation demonstrating your understanding of each reading strategy. Choose a text, present some information about that text (author, context, source), explain why a particular reading style is appropriate for it, demonstrate the reading technique and discuss the insights you gained through that approach.

CHAPTER 2

The basics of reading comprehension

IN THIS CHAPTER

Definition of reading comprehension
The importance of reading comprehension
Different levels of reading comprehension
Strategies for improving reading comprehension

Reading comprehension is the ability to understand the meaning of a text. It is a complex skill that involves several different cognitive processes, such as decoding words, understanding grammar, making inferences and evaluating the text.

Definition of reading comprehension

Reading comprehension is the ability to understand the meaning of a text. This includes understanding the literal meaning of the text, as well as the implied meaning. It also involves understanding the text's structure and organisation, and the author's purpose.

The importance of reading comprehension

Reading comprehension is essential for academic success and for participating in a literate society. At school, without the ability to comprehend what is read, you would struggle to learn new subjects, form opinions, engage in debates and acquire problem-solving skills. It's no exaggeration to say that the ability to understand written text is critical for your academic success and to become a lifelong learner.

Beyond school, though, reading comprehension is equally essential. It allows people to follow instructions, understand contracts, stay informed about current events, enjoy books and literature, and perform many daily tasks. It enables individuals to participate fully in society, equipping them with the knowledge necessary to make informed decisions, whether they're voting, managing their health or avoiding getting scammed.

Different levels of reading comprehension

There are three different levels of reading comprehension: literal, inferential and evaluative.

- **Literal comprehension** is the ability to understand the basic facts and details of a text. This includes understanding the meaning of words, sentences and paragraphs.

- **Inferential comprehension** is the ability to go beyond the literal meaning of the text and make inferences. This includes understanding the author's purpose, drawing conclusions and making predictions.

- **Evaluative comprehension** is the ability to critically evaluate a text. This includes assessing the author's argument, identifying bias and evaluating the text's overall quality.

Strategies for improving reading comprehension

There are several strategies that can be used to improve reading comprehension. These include:

- **Pre-reading:** Before you read a text, it's helpful to preview it. This can be done by reading the title, scanning the headings and looking at the illustrations. Previewing will help you to get a general understanding of what the text is about and to identify the key concepts.

- **Active reading:** When you are reading, it's important to be an active reader. This means that you should be thinking about what you are reading and asking yourself questions. You should also be making connections between the text and your own knowledge and experience.

- **Post-reading:** After you have finished reading, it's helpful to reflect on what you have read. This can be done by summarising the text, discussing it with others or writing about it. Reflecting on what you have read will help you to solidify your understanding of the text.

Activity: Reading detective

Learning intention: To enhance and practise literal, inferential and evaluative comprehension skills.

Instructions:

1. **Step one – Literal comprehension:** Select a text and write down five facts or details directly stated in the text. Be sure to refer to the text to ensure your answers are accurate.

2. **Step two – Inferential comprehension:** Write down three inferences you can make based on the text. These could be about the characters' feelings, motivations or future actions. Remember that your inferences should be supported by evidence from the text.

3. **Step three – Evaluative comprehension:** Write a short paragraph evaluating the text. This could be an opinion about the characters or plot, a critique of the author's writing style or an analysis of the themes or moral of the story. Justify your evaluations with specific examples from the text.

Extension: Comprehension review poster

Create a visual poster or presentation (PowerPoint, Canva) that represents the three levels of comprehension. Use quotes, images, diagrams and your personal interpretations from the text you read to demonstrate literal, inferential and evaluative comprehension.

CHAPTER 3

Developing your vocabulary

IN THIS CHAPTER

The importance of vocabulary in reading comprehension

Strategies for vocabulary acquisition

Vocabulary is an essential part of reading comprehension. The more words you know, the better you will be able to understand what you are reading. In this chapter, we will explore the importance of developing your vocabulary, as well as some strategies for learning new words.

The importance of vocabulary in reading comprehension

Vocabulary is the foundation of reading comprehension. Without a strong vocabulary, it is difficult to understand the meaning of words, sentences and paragraphs. This can make it challenging to follow the plot of a story, understand the main points of an article or complete a research paper.

Vocabulary is essential for academic success. In every subject area, there are specialised words that you need to know to understand the material. For example, in Science, you need to know words like 'hypothesis', 'theory' and 'molecule'. In History, you need to know words like 'revolution', 'colonisation' and 'manifest destiny'.

Strategies for vocabulary acquisition

There are many strategies that you can use to improve your vocabulary. Here are a few of the most effective:

- **Read widely and frequently.** The more you read, the more words you will be exposed to. As you read, pay attention to unfamiliar words, and look them up in a dictionary or thesaurus.

- **Use context clues.** Context clues are hints that authors give to help readers understand the meaning of unfamiliar words. For example, if you read the sentence 'The jubilant crowd cheered as the team won the championship', you can infer that the word 'jubilant' means 'happy' or 'excited'.

- **Learn word roots, prefixes and suffixes.** Many English words are made up of smaller parts, such as roots, prefixes and suffixes. By learning the meaning of these parts, you can figure out the meaning of new words that you encounter. For example, the word 'rejection' is made up of the root 'ject' (to throw), the prefix 're-' (again) and the suffix 'ion' (action). This tells us that 'rejection' is the action of throwing something away again.

- **Use vocabulary games and apps.** There are many vocabulary games and apps available that can make learning new words fun and engaging. These games can help you to memorise new words and to learn how to use them in context.

- **Keep a vocabulary journal.** In a vocabulary journal, you can write down new words that you learn, along with their definitions and examples of how they are used in context. This can be a helpful way to review new words and to practise using them in your own writing.

Activity: Vocabulary hunt

Learning intention: To enhance the vocabulary development and understanding of context clues, roots, prefixes and suffixes.

Instructions:

1. **Step one – Word hunt:** Using the text you're studying, find five new words that you are unfamiliar with. Write down each word and the sentence it appears in.
2. **Step two – Dissecting words:** For each new word, try to break it down into its prefix, root and suffix.
3. **Step three – Guess the meaning:** Based on the word's context in the sentence, and the parts of the word, try to guess the meaning of the word.
4. **Step four – Look it up:** After making your best guess, look up the word in a dictionary or online to find its actual meaning. Compare the actual meaning to the meaning you came up with.
5. **Step five – Create a vocab card:** On a flashcard or a piece of paper, write down the word, its definition, the sentence it came from and its prefix, root and suffix (if applicable). Also include your initial guess of the word's meaning for reference.
6. **Step six – Share with peers:** Share your findings with a classmate or group. This will help you to learn the new words your mates found and help them learn the new words you found.

Extension: Vocabulary in action

Select three words from your vocabulary hunt flashcards and incorporate them into a short story or paragraph. The aim is not just to use the words, but to contextually demonstrate their meaning. After this writing task, gather into groups with your friends and classmates and exchange your written pieces. Assess how effectively the words were used, ensuring they align with the actual meanings and are clear in context.

Reading at school

CHAPTER 4

Reading strategies for textbooks

IN THIS CHAPTER

Previewing a textbook
Navigating graphs, charts and sidebars
Taking notes from textbooks

Reading textbooks effectively is an integral skill for high school. No doubt you've got a backpack full of textbooks that you *must* read. Reading and understanding textbooks can be a challenging task due to their dense, information-heavy content, varied layouts and specialised vocabulary. Textbooks are a major source of information for your high school studies, so it is important to have some strategies in place to help you maximise your understanding.

Previewing a textbook

Before jumping straight into the reading of a textbook, it's beneficial to spend some time previewing the content. This involves looking at the material to understand its content and structure. The textbook you're using may develop in stages, meaning that chapter three needs to be read before chapter four, otherwise you won't get the material in chapter four. Here are some steps to follow, which will help you gain an understanding of your textbook:

1. **Know your purpose:** Before jumping in, figure out exactly what you need to find out from the textbook. Identify what you need to learn or what you want to get out of reading the book. This will help focus you and keep you engaged.

2. **Examine the table of contents:** This seems an obvious starting point, but sometimes you'll just go to the page your teacher tells you to. By viewing the table of contents, you will be able to get a clear idea of how the book is organised and what topics are covered. Pay attention to the headings and subheadings as they outline the main themes and sub-themes.

3. **Read the introduction and conclusion:** These sections provide a summary of what the book aims to teach and the main conclusions or findings. They set the stage for the detailed content to follow.

4. **Review chapter summaries and review questions:** These sections will help you understand the key takeaways from each chapter and the questions you should be able to answer after the reading. They're also the homework you'll likely be set by your teacher!

Navigating graphs, charts and sidebars

Textbooks often include visual aids such as graphs, charts and sidebars that provide additional information or illustrate the text's concepts. Learning how to navigate these features is an essential part of textbook reading.

1. **Ask questions:** When you come across a graph, chart or sidebar, ask yourself questions like 'What is this showing me?' or 'How does this relate to the main text?' Asking questions will help you make sense of the visual information and connect it to the rest of the text.

2. **Pay attention to visual aids:** Don't just skip over graphs or charts. Take time to understand what they are showing, read the captions and see how they relate to the text. Read the text before and after the graphics to really unpack what's happening.

3. **Use sidebars:** Sidebars often contain additional information, definitions or interesting facts related to the main text. Make sure to read them to enrich your understanding of the topic. These sidebars sometimes have the definitions of keywords and phrases – these can help with your understanding of the text and help with any revision you may need to do.

Taking notes from textbooks

Note-taking is an active reading strategy that can significantly enhance comprehension and retention. Note-taking isn't simply copying the material verbatim from the text – you need to be able to understand the textbook in your own, unique way.

1. **Be selective:** Don't try to write down everything. Focus on key concepts, facts, definitions and arguments. Use the textbook's structure (headings, subheadings, bold or italicised text) to guide your note-taking.

2. **Use your own words:** I mentioned this before. Paraphrase the content instead of copying verbatim. This ensures that you're processing the information, not just transcribing it.

3. **Organise your notes:** Use headings, subheadings, bullet points and diagrams to organise your notes. This makes it easier for you to review later.

4. **Review your notes:** Now that you've got all your notes, take some time to review them to make sure you understand the material. You can also use these notes to study for your exams, so make sure they're tip-top.

Activity: Textbook exploration

Learning intention: To practise previewing a textbook, navigating visual aids and taking effective notes.

Instructions:

1. **Step one – Previewing:** Spend 10–15 minutes previewing a textbook. Write down the book's main topics (from the table of contents) and the key points from the introduction and conclusion. Also, note down any interesting or surprising information you find.

2. **Step two – Visual aids:** Find a chapter with several graphs, charts or sidebars. Spend some time studying each visual aid and sidebar. Write down what each one is about and how it contributes to your understanding of the text.

3. **Step three – Note-taking:** Choose a section of the textbook (a few pages) to read in detail. This could be the homework you've been assigned. As you read, take notes focusing on the key points, using your own words. Use headings or bullet points to organise your notes.

4. **Step four – Review and reflect:** Review your notes and reflect on the reading and note-taking process. Did previewing the book help your understanding? Were the visual aids and sidebars useful? Were your notes clear and helpful? Make a list of what worked well and what you could improve for next time.

Extension: Creating a chapter summary

Choose a chapter from your textbook. It can be the same one you worked on during the textbook exploration activity above. Using your preview notes, insights from visual aids and detailed reading notes, create a summary of the chapter. This should include key points, significant details from visual aids and your own interpretations and reflections.

CHAPTER 5

Reading strategies for literature

IN THIS CHAPTER

Identifying themes and motifs

Recognising plot, setting, characters and conflicts

Analysing symbolism and other literary devices

Reading literature can be a rewarding experience, but it can also be challenging due to the complex themes, intricate plotlines, multifaceted characters and various literary devices. To enhance your understanding and appreciation of literature, here are some strategies to employ.

Identifying themes and motifs

English and Literature teachers love to bang on about the themes of the text. I would know, I am one. But what exactly is the theme of a text? A theme is a central idea or message that the author seeks to convey in a literary work, while a motif is a recurring element that supports the theme.

1. **Look beyond the surface:** A theme is not always explicitly stated; instead, it's often implied. Think about what the story is trying to tell you beyond the plot. Some examples of themes in major literary works include:

    a. **Love:** *Romeo and Juliet, The Great Gatsby, Pride and Prejudice*
    b. **Loss:** *The Catcher in the Rye, The Fault in Our Stars, To Kill a Mockingbird*
    c. **Redemption:** *The Shawshank Redemption, Les Misérables, The Alchemist*

2. **Note recurring elements:** If you notice a word, phrase, image or idea recurring in the story, it's likely a motif that contributes to the theme. Pay attention to these repetitive elements and consider their significance. Some examples of motifs from literary works include:

    a. **Red rose:** *The Scarlet Letter, Beauty and the Beast*
    b. **Water:** *The Great Gatsby, Moby Dick, The Lord of the Rings*
    c. **Eyes:** *The Eyes of Tammy Faye, The Picture of Dorian Gray, The Fault in Our Stars*

Recognising plot, setting, characters and conflicts

These are the fundamental elements of a story and recognising them can significantly enhance your understanding of the text.

1. **Plot:** This is the sequence of events that make up the story. As you read, try and identify:

    a. *The exposition:* the introduction to the story, where the characters and the setting are introduced.

    b. *The rising action:* The part of the story where the conflict is introduced, and the stakes are raised.

    c. *The climax:* The turning point of the story, where the conflict is resolved.

    d. *The falling action:* The part of the story where conflict is resolved and the story is coming to a close.

    e. *The resolution:* The end of the story, where the characters have learned and grown because of their experiences.

2. **Setting:** The setting includes both the time and place of the story.

    a. It can be important to the story because it can influence the characters' actions and motivations. For example, in *The Great Gatsby*, the setting of the Roaring Twenties is important because it reflects the characters' sense of decadence and excess.

3. **Characters:** They are the people in the story.
   a. There can be main characters, who drive the plot, and secondary characters, who support the main characters.
   b. It is important to identify the characters' traits, motivations and changes throughout the story. This will help you to understand their actions and motivations. For example, in *To Kill a Mockingbird*, Scout Finch is a young girl who learns to see the world through the eyes of others.

4. **Conflicts:** Conflicts are the problems that characters face in the story.
   a. Conflicts can be internal (within a character) or external (between characters, or between a character and an external force).
   b. Conflicts drive the plot and influence character development. Also, generally when there's conflict, the text's themes, ideas and values are being explored. Pay attention to who/what wins the conflict.

Analysing symbolism and other literary devices

Authors often use literary devices such as symbolism, metaphor, simile and allusion to add depth and richness to their work. Remember: the curtain isn't just blue; the curtain symbolises the melancholy state of the character (English teachers love this stuff!).

1. **Symbolism:** This is when an object, action, word, character or event represents something else. Try to identify symbols and consider their meanings in the context of the story.

2. **Metaphor and simile:** These compare two things and create a vivid picture or idea. Identify these comparisons and consider what they contribute to the story.

3. **Allusion:** This is a reference to another work of literature, person or event. Recognise these references to deepen your understanding of the text.

4. **Other literary devices:** There are many other literary devices that can be used to create meaning in a text. Some common devices include imagery, figurative language, foreshadowing and irony. It is important to be aware of these devices and how they can be used to enhance your understanding of a text.

Activity: Literature professor

Learning intention: To practise identifying themes and motifs, recognising story elements and analysing literary devices.

Instructions:

1. **Step one – Theme and motif:** Read through a story or chapter once without stopping. Write down what you think the theme(s) might be. Also, note any recurring elements that could be motifs.

2. **Step two – Story elements:** Re-read the story or chapter. This time, pause to note down the plot (including its main stages), the setting, the characters (and their traits, motivations and changes) and any conflicts.

3. **Step three – Literary devices:** Read through the story or chapter a third time. Look for symbols, metaphors, similes and allusions. Write down each one you find, along with what you think it means or represents.

4. **Step four – Reflection:** Review your notes. Reflect on how the theme, motifs, story elements and literary devices contribute to the overall story. Write a summary of your thoughts.

Extension: Literature writer

You've played the part of professor, now play the part of author! Building on the skills developed in the activity above, apply your understanding of themes, motifs, story elements and literary devices to create your own short story.

CHAPTER 6

Reading strategies for Maths

IN THIS CHAPTER

Strategies for reading mathematically

Reading in Maths is just as important as it is in English and Literature. Maths is a language, and like any language, it takes practice to read and understand it fluently. Now, I know that most of the things you read in Maths are numbers, and x, and y, and equations, and Pythagoras (can you tell I'm not a Maths teacher?), but there are words as well. You will come up against worded questions in your Maths texts and exams. Like that dude who buys 1 million bananas and must travel 30km on two trains leaving different cities… you get the idea. Here are some strategies that can help you read and comprehend Maths texts more effectively.

Strategies for reading mathematically

1. **Preview the text.** Before you start reading, take a few minutes to preview and skim over the text. This means looking at the title, headings, subheadings and any visuals. This will give you a general idea of what the text is about and what you can expect to learn.

2. **Identify the key vocabulary.** Pay attention to the key vocabulary in the text. This includes words that are important to the understanding of the text, as well as words that you're not familiar with. If you come across a word that you don't know, take a moment to look it up. As you learn new words, build yourself a mathematical lexicon. Create flashcards or maintain a glossary in your book.

3. **Chunk information.** Much like reading a novel, chunking involves breaking down information into manageable parts. In Maths, this could mean:
    a. Separating a complex problem into distinct steps
    b. Grouping like terms
    c. Dividing long equations at equal signs or other important operators

4. **Visualising.** For many, Maths concepts become clearer when visualised. Graphs, number lines, geometric drawings and even physical manipulatives can make abstract ideas tangible. When reading a Maths problem or concept, consider:
   a. Sketching diagrams or figures
   b. Drawing charts or graphs
   c. Using colour coding to differentiate variables and operations

5. **Active engagement.** Passively reading a mathematic textbook or notes isn't enough. Actively engage with the material by:
   a. Writing out problems
   b. Solving sample problems without looking at solutions
   c. Explaining concepts aloud or teaching them to someone else

6. **Real-world applications.** Maths is everywhere. Connect Maths concepts to real-world situations so you can enhance your understanding and retention. For example, relate algebra to budgeting or geometry to architecture.

Reading in Maths is a skill that, like any other, improves with practice. With the right strategies, you can navigate mathematic texts and problems more effectively, leading to a better understanding and appreciation of the subject. Remember, every mathematical problem tells a story, and with the right approach, you can understand and, perhaps, enjoy it.

Activity: Mathematical storytelling

Learning intention: To reinforce strategies for Maths and demonstrate an understanding and application of Maths problems in real-world scenarios.

Instructions:

1. **Step one – Select a math topic:** Choose a mathematic concept or theorem you've recently studied or found interesting.

2. **Step two – Research real-world applications:** Based on the concept chosen, research real-world application or scenarios where this Maths idea is important.

3. **Step three – Craft a word problem:** Using your research, craft a word problem that embeds the chosen mathematic concept within a real-life scenario. Your problem should be detailed and use the relevant Maths vocabulary.

4. **Step four – Visualising:** Accompany your word problem with a relevant diagram, graph or illustration that provides a visual context.

5. **Step five – Chunking breakdown:** On a separate piece of paper, break down the solution to your problem into distinct, manageable steps.

Extension: Maths narratives

Craft a short fictional narrative centred on your chosen Maths concept. Within your story, integrate two to three maths problems related to the concept, which readers must solve to advance the plot. Share your narrative with a friend, allowing them to tackle the embedded questions, then discuss their solutions.

CHAPTER 7

Reading strategies for Science

IN THIS CHAPTER

Understanding the structure of scientific texts
Strategies for scientific reading

Reading in Science, whether it's a textbook, research paper or news article, often requires a different set of strategies and language compared with other subjects. Like Maths, Science has its own language. Scientific content can be dense, filled with jargon and often requires you to process complex information or grapple with weird and unfamiliar concepts. This chapter gives you some strategies to help you navigate the scientific world and the texts you'll come across a little easier.

Understanding the structure of scientific texts

1. **Research papers:** These are often structured in the IMRaD format: introduction, methods, results and discussion. Each section has its own purpose, and knowing each purpose will help you get what's going on:

   a. *Introduction* sets the stage and states the research questions.

   b. *Methods* describes the experiment's set-up.

   c. *Results* presents the data and the findings.

   d. *Discussion* interprets the results in a broader context, sometimes posing new or different research questions.

2. **Textbooks:** Chapters usually start with objectives, followed by explanations, examples and diagrams, and end with a summary.

3. **Review articles:** Review articles provide a comprehensive overview of a specific field of science. They summarise the current state of understanding on a topic. Unlike research papers, which report new findings, review articles analyse previously published studies to give readers a wide-ranging view on the topic. They're generally structured like this:

   a. *Abstract:* A brief overview of what the review covers.

   b. *Introduction:* Introduces the topic and states the purpose of the review.

   c. *Background:* Some contexts about the field or subject of the review.

d. *Main body:* This section is typically broken down into subheadings relevant to the topic. It's where most of the previous research is discussed:
   i. *Subtopics:* Each subtopic covers a specific area of the wider topic.
   ii. *Comparative analyses:* Discusses the differences and similarities in findings from the different studies.
e. *Discussion/conclusion:* Summarises the main points discussed, highlights gaps in current knowledge and may suggest areas for future research.
f. *References:* Lists all the studies and papers referenced in the review.

4. **Case studies:** Case studies are detailed examinations of specific subjects (like a patient or a particular event) to glean insights or draw broader conclusions. They're generally structured like this:
   a. *Abstract:* Outlines the main points and findings of the case study.
   b. *Introduction:* Introduces the subject and gives you some background information.
   c. *Case presentation:* Detailed description of the specific case or subject being studied.
   d. *Intervention and outcome:* Describes any actions taken and the results of those actions.
   e. *Discussion:* Places the specific case in a broader context. Discusses what can be learned from the case.
   f. *Conclusions:* Summarises the findings and their implications.
   g. *References:* Cites any relevant literature or studies related to the case.

Strategies for scientific reading

- **Active engagement**
  - *Highlight and annotate:* As you read, underline key terms, and annotate the margins with summaries, questions or connections to prior knowledge.
  - *Concept maps:* These visual aids can help you understand relationships between different ideas. As you read, sketch out a concept map that links major ideas.

- **Focus on vocabulary**
  - *Build a glossary:* Create your own glossary. For each term, write a definition in your own words and draw a picture or diagram.
  - *Flashcards:* To help you retain information, turn these into flashcards and review periodically.

- **Visuals are vital**
  - *Analyse graphics:* Diagrams, graphs and charts are integral in Science. Before reading the text, examine any visuals. Try to interpret what they represent.

- **Summarise and paraphrase**
  - After reading a section, take some time to summarise the main points in your own words. This will help you to further comprehend and will help you retain the information.

- **Practise critical reading**
  - *Evaluate sources:* Science requires a sceptical mind. Consider the credibility of the author and the publication. Is it peer-reviewed?
  - *Question conclusions:* Just because something is in print doesn't make it irrefutable. Does the data support the conclusions?

Approaching scientific texts with a methodical and active strategy can help you improve your comprehension and dominate in your assessments and exams. Like all skills, you need to practice. Don't just do it once and move on. Science is an exploration of the unknown and with the right reading strategies, you can join in on the journey of discovery.

Activity: Navigating scientific text structures

Learning intention: To help you get to grips with different scientific text structures and further develop your skills in extracting relevant information.

Instructions:

1. **Review article analysis**
   a. Source a review article (online or from your teacher, or the one you've been given to read for homework).
   b. Identify and highlight the different sections of the article.
   c. Within the main body, identify and note down the various subtopics discussed.
   d. Summarise each section in your own words.

2. **Case study analysis**
   a. Again, use the one you've already been given, or find one online.
   b. Identify and highlight the different sections.
   c. Pay close attention to the 'case presentation' and 'intervention and outcome' sections. Extract the key details and findings.
   d. Summarise the case's primary insights and their relevance to broader scientific contexts.

3. **Discussion**
   a. Discuss the main findings from the review article and/or the case study.
   b. Consider the advantages and limitations of each structure. For example, how does a review article's broad overview compare with the in-depth focus of a case study.

Extension: Present your findings

Create a brief presentation of infographics comparing the structures. There are some cool websites with preloaded templates around that can help – try Canva, for example. Include key components for each, their purposes and potential audiences. Provide real-world examples of when and why a scientist might choose one form over the other.

Reading in the real world

CHAPTER 8
Critical reading skills

IN THIS CHAPTER

Understanding bias and perspective
Evaluating sources and information
Distinguishing fact from opinion

Information is everywhere. In our information-rich society, being able to read critically is an important skill – especially now with the rise of AI, fake news, deepfakes, trolls, misinformation, etc. Critical reading involves more than just understanding text; it's about analysing and evaluating the information, understanding the source's perspective, and distinguishing between fact and opinion. Let's dive into these aspects further.

Understanding bias and perspective

Everyone has biases, which are influences that impact our thinking and decision-making processes. When you read, it's important to understand that the author's perspective might be influenced by certain biases. Some examples of how bias can influence the way we read and interpret information include:

- People who are pro-life may be more likely to see a foetus as a human being with rights, while people who are pro-choice may see a foetus as a clump of cells.

- People who live in a wealthy neighbourhood may be more likely to see poverty because of laziness, while people who live in a poor neighbourhood may be more likely to believe that poverty is a result of systemic inequality.

So, how do you identify bias in a text? Well, I've got some ideas for you:

1. **The words:** Look for words or phrases that indicate bias, such as 'always', 'never', 'most' or 'only'.

2. **Tone and language:** Pay attention to the author's tone and language. Does the author seem to be trying to persuade you to believe something?

3. **Recognise the author's point of view:** Consider who the author is, their background and possible motivations for writing. This can help you understand their perspective. What is the author's agenda?

4. **Identify potential bias:** Look for indications of bias, such as one-sided arguments, emotional language or selective use of facts. Remember that bias isn't always negative; it just means that the author has a certain perspective.

It is important to be aware of our own biases so that we can take steps to overcome them. We can start by questioning ourselves, and what our beliefs are on a certain topic, or group of people. Consider your assumptions about the world. Once we've identified our biases, we can start to challenge them. We can do this by reading about different perspectives, talking to people with different beliefs and being open to new information.

Evaluating sources and information

Not all sources of information are equally reliable. Critical reading involves assessing the credibility of the source and the quality of the information.

1. **Assess the source:** Consider the source's reputation, expertise and potential biases. Is the source generally considered reliable and credible?

    a. Some reputable sources include:
        i. News organisations with a history of accuracy and fairness, such as *ABC News*, *The New York Times*, *The Washington Post* and *The Guardian*
        ii. Academic articles that have been peer-reviewed
        iii. Government websites that are official and up to date

    b. Some unreliable sources include:
        i. Blogs and websites that are not associated with a reputable organisation
        ii. Social media posts from people who are not experts in the topic being discussed
        iii. Websites that are known for spreading dis- and misinformation

2. **Evaluate the information:** Look at the evidence provided to support the information or arguments. Is it based on facts, research or reputable sources? Are opposing viewpoints considered?

It is important to use multiple sources of information to verify what you're reading about. No single source is always 100% accurate. When you're researching a topic, try to find sources from different perspectives. This will help you to get a more balanced view of the issue. There are also a range of fact-checking websites out there to help you see through all the noise.

Distinguishing fact from opinion

You will encounter people in your life that consider their opinion to be 100% verifiable fact. Well, most of the time it's not, and you should probably call them out on that. Here's how to do that. Put simply, a *fact* is a statement that can be proven to be true or false. An *opinion* is a subjective belief that varies from person to person.

1. **Identify facts:** Facts are typically objective and verifiable. They often contain precise details or statistics and are supported by evidence. Facts are statements that can be proven true or false. For example, 'the Earth is round' is a fact.

2. **Recognise opinions:** Opinions are subjective and may be influenced by personal feelings or beliefs. They might contain words like 'believe', 'think', 'feel' or 'seem'. An example of an opinion might be 'coriander tastes good'. (Which it doesn't, it tastes like soap – well, that's my opinion anyway!)

It is important to be able to distinguish between facts and opinions because it can help us to make informed decisions and to avoid being misled by misinformation. Facts are based on evidence, while opinions aren't. When you're making decisions, it's important to base them on facts.

Activity: Critical reading challenge

Learning intention: To practise understanding bias and perspective, evaluating sources and information, and distinguishing fact from opinion.

Instructions:

1. **Step one – Gather your texts:** Find a range of articles from a wide variety of sources. Don't just choose the first Google result! Dig around the results and find different voices and perspectives.

2. **Step two – Bias and perspective:** For each article, identify the author and their potential perspective. Write down any indications of bias you notice in the article.

3. **Step three – Evaluating sources and information:** Assess the credibility of each source and the quality of the information provided. Write down the reasons for your assessment.

4. **Step four – Fact or opinion:** For each article, write down three statements that you believe are facts and three that you believe are opinions. Explain your reasoning.

5. **Step five – Reflection:** Compare your findings for the different articles. Did the author's perspective or the source's credibility impact the information presented? Was it easy to distinguish fact from opinion? Consider how this might impact your future reading.

Extension: Debate

Now that you've seen how people argue on the internet, practise arguing with your friends and classmates. Consider staging a debate on one of the topics covered in the articles. This will give you a chance to further develop your critical reading skills and apply them in a dynamic, real-world context.

CHAPTER 9

Reading in the digital age

IN THIS CHAPTER

AI and filter bubbles
Relying on Google searches
Critical evaluation of internet sources
Reading online

The digital age is a remarkable time in human history. It offers a wealth of information and resources right at your fingertips. The internet, smartphones and AI are now part and parcel of the learning environment. This chapter will provide some strategies for exploring these resources effectively and to critically evaluate them, as well as how to adapt your reading strategies to optimise your learning in the digital landscape.

AI and filter bubbles

Artificial intelligence (AI) has become a huge player in the digital information space. AI algorithms are designed to predict and serve content based on what we put into them, our online behaviour, our searches and our interactions. No doubt you've tinkered with ChatGPT, Claude or Bard (don't lie, I know you've used them to smash out your homework!). AI can be helpful in providing us with relevant content, but it can also lead to a phenomenon known as the 'filter bubble'.

A filter bubble is a situation where users are exposed mostly to ideas that align with their existing beliefs, potentially limiting their worldview. This can happen because AI algorithms are trained on our past behaviour, so they are more likely to show us content that we have already liked or interacted with. As a result, we may never be exposed to new or different ideas.

To counter filter bubbles, it is important to be aware of them and to take steps to avoid them. Here are a few tips:

- **Use multiple search engines.** Google is not the only search engine out there, and each one has its own algorithms and biases. By using multiple search engines, you can get a wider range of results.

- **Read different news sources.** Don't just stick to one news source. Read from a variety of sources, including those that you disagree with.

- **Talk to people with different viewpoints.** Talk to your friends, family and neighbours about the news and current events. Get their perspectives on different issues.

By following these tips, you can help to avoid filter bubbles and get a more balanced view of the world.

In addition to the above, I would also add that it is important to be critical of the information that we get from AI algorithms. Just because an algorithm says something is true, doesn't mean that it is. Always fact-check information before you believe it.

Relying on Google searches

Since I've mentioned Google, I might as well dive in deeper. We all love Google. And we all know Google is a powerful tool for finding information, but it is important to be critical of the information that you find. Not all information on the internet is accurate or reliable. And it's important to not click on the first result and take it at face value.

Here are some tips for evaluating the credibility of a website:

- **Check the website's author.** Is the author an expert on the topic? Is the author affiliated with a reputable organisation?
- **Look for typos or grammatical errors.** These can be a sign that the website is not well-maintained or that the information is not accurate.
- **Look for evidence of bias.** Does the website seem to be trying to promote a particular viewpoint? Is the information presented in a balanced way?

Here are some tips for using advanced search options on Google:

- **Use quotation marks** to search for an exact phrase. This will help you to avoid getting results that are just related to the words in the phrase, but not the meaning of the phrase.
- **Use the minus sign** (-) to exclude certain words from your search results. This can be helpful if you are getting a lot of irrelevant results.
- **Use the advanced search page** to filter your results by date, language and other criteria. This can help you to find more relevant results.

It is also important to use multiple sources when doing research. This means getting information from different websites, books and articles. By doing this, you can get a more complete and more accurate picture of the topic you are researching.

Critical evaluation of internet sources

Not all information online is trustworthy. It is important to be critical of the information that you find, and to evaluate the sources carefully. Here are some things to consider when evaluating an internet source:

- **Authority.** Who is the author? What are their qualifications? Is the website affiliated with a reputable organisation?

- **Accuracy.** Is the information presented factual and unbiased? Are there references to back up the claims?

- **Currency.** When was the content last updated? For many topics, especially in the sciences, recent information is crucial.

- **Purpose.** Is the content meant to inform, persuade or sell a product? Beware of biases that could colour the information being presented.

- **Look for typos or grammatical errors.** These can be a sign that the source is not well-maintained or that the information is not accurate.

- **Look for evidence of bias.** Does the source seem to be trying to promote a particular viewpoint? Is the information presented in a balanced way?

- **Use multiple sources.** Get information from different websites, books and articles. By doing this, you can get a more complete and more accurate picture of the topic you are researching.

- **Fact-check information.** If you are unsure about the accuracy of something you have read online, you can use a fact-checking website to verify the information.

Reading online

Reading online or onscreen is different from reading a physical book. Research suggests that people tend to skim more and dive less deeply when reading on a screen. Here are some tips to adapt your reading strategies:

1. **Avoid distractions:** Close unrelated tabs, use full-screen mode and turn off notifications. Consider tools that block distracting websites.

2. **Highlight and annotate:** Use digital tools for highlighting text and making notes. However, avoid over-highlighting, which can reduce effectiveness.

3. **Take breaks:** Avoid screen fatigue by taking regular breaks. Get up and move around every 20–30 minutes to avoid screen fatigue. You can also try using a blue light filter to reduce strain on your eyes.

4. **Read slowly and deliberately:** Don't try to speed-read text on a screen. Take your time and make sure you understand what you're reading.

5. **Read actively:** Ask yourself questions as you read and make connections to your own knowledge and experience.

6. **Use a variety of sources:** Don't just rely on one source of information when you're reading online. Get information from a variety of sources to get a well-rounded view of the topic.

Activity: Evaluating online sources

Learning intention: To develop your abilities to evaluate online sources, discerning high-quality, reliable information from less credible content.

Instructions:

1. Choose a topic you're interested in.

2. Search for information online; find three sources – one that you believe is highly credible, one of questionable credibility and one that you think is not credible.

3. Apply the critical evaluation criteria (authority, accuracy, currency and purpose) to each of these sources.

4. Write a short paragraph explaining your evaluation of each source.

5. Discuss your findings with a classmate or the teacher. Do they agree with your evaluations? Why or why not?

Extension: Annotated bibliography

This is the kind of assignment you might do at university or TAFE. Look at you go! Create an annotated bibliography on a topic of your choice. This will require you to find and critically evaluate a larger number of sources, summarising the key points and assessing the sources' credibility.

CHAPTER 10

Improving reading speed and efficiency

IN THIS CHAPTER

Techniques for speed-reading

Avoiding subvocalization

Speed and efficiency are essential to maximise the values of your reading time. Whether you're studying for a test, reading a book for pleasure or catching up on the news, being able to read quickly and effectively can be a significant advantage. This chapter will introduce you to techniques for speed-reading, ways to avoid subvocalization, and methods for developing eye movement and visual span.

Techniques for speed-reading

Speed-reading involves reading at an increased speed without a significant loss in comprehension. Here are a few strategies to help improve your reading speed:

- **Chunking:** Instead of reading word by word, try to read groups of words. Your eyes can perceive multiple words at once, allowing you to take in more information in a single glance. For example, instead of reading 'the quick brown fox', try to read 'thequickbrownfox'.

- **Minimising regressions:** Regressions occur when your eyes move backward to reread text. Try to reduce this habit by using your finger or a pen to guide your reading. This will help you to keep your eyes moving forward and prevent you from regressing.

- **Skimming and scanning:** Skimming involves quickly looking over a text to get a general sense of the content. Scanning, on the other hand, is looking for specific information. Both are effective ways to read text quickly when deep comprehension is not necessary.

- **Practise regularly:** The more you practise, the better you will become at speed-reading.

- **Use a timer:** Set a timer for a certain amount of time and see how much text you can read in that time. This will help you to track your progress and set new goals.

- **Vary your reading speed:** Don't try to speed-read all the time. Sometimes it is better to read slowly and carefully to ensure that you understand the material.

- **Take breaks:** Don't try to speed-read for hours on end. Your eyes and brain need a break every 20–30 minutes.

Avoiding subvocalization

Subvocalization is the habit of silently pronouncing each word in your head as you read it. While it can aid comprehension, it also slows your reading speed down. There are a few things you can do to reduce subvocalization:

- **Be conscious of it.** When you notice yourself subvocalizing, try to stop and focus on the meaning of the text rather than the individual words.

- **Practise reading without subvocalizing.** Start by reading short passages and gradually increase the length of the passages as you become more comfortable.

- **Try reading aloud.** This can help you to break the habit of subvocalizing in your head.

- **Chew gum or hum softly while reading.** This can help distract the part of your brain that wants to subvocalize words.

It is important to be patient and persistent when trying to reduce subvocalization. It can take time and practise to break the habit. However, the benefits of reducing subvocalization are worth it. You will be able to read faster and with greater comprehension.

Activity: Practising speed-reading

Learning intention: This activity will enable you to apply and assess speed-reading techniques, helping you to identify effective strategies to improve your reading speed.

Instructions:

1. Select a piece of text to practise with. Start with something relatively easy and increase the complexity as your skills improve.

2. Time yourself reading the text normally.

3. Practise chunking. Read the same text again, but try to take in groups of words at a time rather than reading word by word.

4. Read the text again, this time actively avoiding subvocalization. You might find it helpful to chew gum or hum softly while reading.

5. Finally, focus on your eye movements. Try to minimise regressions and expand your visual span.

6. After each step, time yourself again to see if your speed has improved.

7. Make note of what techniques worked best for you and what you found challenging.

Extension – Speed-reading challenge

Let's make this quick (see what I did there?!). Select a relatively easy piece of text and apply the speed-reading techniques. As you read, summarise the main points of the text – this will ensure you've also maintained comprehension.

CHAPTER 11

Developing a reading habit

IN THIS CHAPTER

Finding the right books

Setting a reading schedule

The role of libraries and book clubs

Fostering a reading habit can transform your life. Reading expands your horizons, fuels your imagination, boosts your knowledge, and improves your comprehension and writing skills. This chapter will guide you on developing a consistent reading habit, finding the right books, setting a reading schedule, and leveraging resources like libraries and book clubs.

Finding the right books

The journey towards a consistent reading habit often begins with finding the right books. The 'right book' differs for everyone and depends on your interests, reading level and the goals you have for your reading.

- **Align with your interests:** Choose books on topics you're passionate about or curious to learn. If you love science fiction movies, consider books in that genre. If you're interested in history, biographies of historical figures or historical novels might intrigue you.

- **Suitable reading level:** Select books that match your reading level. If a book is too challenging, it might annoy you; if it's too easy, it might bore you. The right level is slightly challenging but still enjoyable and readable.

- **Book recommendations:** Use online platforms like Goodreads or websites with book reviews and recommendations. Ask teachers, friends or family for book suggestions. Don't forget your teachers – they read books, too! Keep an ongoing list of books you want to read.

Setting a reading schedule

Consistency is key to developing any habit, and reading is no different. A reading schedule can be instrumental in making reading a part of your daily routine.

1. **Dedicated reading time:** Set aside dedicated time for reading each day. It could be in the morning to kickstart your day, in the evening to unwind or any time you can consistently commit.

2. **Start small:** Begin with as little as 15–20 minutes a day. As you get comfortable, gradually increase the time.

3. **Consistency over quantity:** It's more beneficial to read a little each day than to read for hours one day and then not at all for a few days. The goal is to make a daily reading habit.

The role of libraries and book clubs

Libraries and book clubs offer supportive communities and resources that can enrich your reading habit.

1. **Libraries:** Libraries provide access to a vast array of books, often for free. They usually have knowledgeable staff that can guide you in finding books you'll enjoy. Many libraries also offer digital resources, include eBooks and audio books.

2. **Book clubs:** Book clubs can make reading a social activity. They introduce you to books and perspectives you might not encounter on your own. The discussion and analysis in book clubs can enhance your understanding and appreciation of the book.

Conclusion

Reading is not an isolated skill. It interconnects with various aspects of our academic, professional and personal lives. Two of the most crucial skills that are intimately connected with reading are writing and critical thinking. Reading also impacts our communication abilities.

The links between reading and writing

Reading and writing are two sides of the same coin. Reading and writing are essential skills for school, work and life. They are closely linked. Reading helps improve your writing and writing helps improve your reading. Here are some of the ways that these two skills are interlinked:

1. **Grammar and sentence structure:** Reading helps you understand how sentences are structured and how grammar is used in practice. It's a form of implicit learning where you subconsciously absorb grammatical rules and sentence structures, which you can then apply in your own writing.

2. **Understanding genres and styles:** Reading various genres and styles can help you understand their unique characteristics. Recognising these elements can inspire and guide your writing, helping you to develop your voice and style.

3. **Ideas development:** Reading allows you to see how authors develop ideas, build arguments and create compelling narratives. It serves as a model for organising your thoughts and presenting them effectively in your writing.

4. **Helping you develop a sense of audience:** When you read, you are constantly thinking about who the author is writing for and what they are trying to achieve. This, in turn, helps you to think about the purpose of your own writing.

5. **Giving you a sense of purpose:** When you read, you are transported to another world and immersed in a story. This can be a great escape from the trials of everyday life and will also give you inspiration for your own writing.

The relationship between reading and communication and critical thinking

Reading has a huge impact on your communication and critical thinking skills. You probably don't even realise it, but here are some of the ways that reading changes the way you think and the way you speak:

- **Increased vocabulary:** Reading exposes you to a wider range of vocabulary than you would typically encounter in everyday conversation. This helps you to better understand and express yourself when you speak and/or write.

- **Improved comprehension:** Reading helps you to develop your comprehension skills, which are essential for understanding and responding to complex texts. If you read regularly, you become better at following an author's argument, identifying the main points of a text and drawing inferences.

- **Enhanced critical thinking skills:** Reading helps you to develop your critical thinking skills, such as the ability to evaluate information, identify bias and form your own opinions. When you read critically, you are not simply accepting the information that you are presented with. Instead, you are actively analysing the text and thinking about its meaning.

- **Better writing skills:** Reading helps you to develop better writing skills by exposing you to different writing styles and techniques. If you read regularly, you are better able to organise your thoughts, write clearly and concisely, and use effective grammar and punctuation.

- **Improved listening skills:** Reading helps you to improve your listening skills by teaching you how to focus your attention and follow a speaker's argument. When you read regularly, you are better able to listen to others and understand their points of view.

On top of all that, reading also helps you to develop a better understanding of the world around you. By reading about different cultures, historical events and scientific discoveries, you gain a broader perspective on life. This helps you to become a more informed citizen and make better choices in life.

So, where to start with all of this? Here are some tips for improving your communication and critical thinking skills by reading:

- **Choose books that are challenging but not too difficult.** You should be able to understand the main point of the book, but you should also be challenged to think critically about the text. Next time you go to the library, don't just grab a book that has a large font and pictures.
- **Read a variety of genres.** This will help you to develop a broad range of reading skills.
- **Read actively.** This means paying attention to the text, asking questions and making connections to your own life and experiences.
- **Discuss what you read with others.** This can help you to clarify your understanding of the text and develop your own ideas.
- **Write about what you read.** This will help you to solidify your understanding of the text and to communicate your ideas with others.